CONQUER SERIES

Study Guide
Volume 1

For Individual or Small Group Study

Jeremy & Tiana Wiles
with Heather Kolb

In collaboration with:
Dr. Ted Roberts
Bryan Roberts
Harry Flanagan
Linda Dodge
Sauna Winsor

D1441525

A KingdomWorks resource for discipleship
KingdomWorks.com

Copyright © 2020 by Jeremy & Tiana Wiles

CONQUER SERIES Study Guide Volume 1
Published by KingdomWorks Studios
2751 SE Monroe St, Stuart, FL 34997 USA
www.kingdomworks.com

All rights reserved. Except as permitted by U.S. Copyright Act of 1976,
no part of this book may be reproduced, distributed or transmitted in
any form or by any means, or stored in a database or retrieval system,
without the prior written permission of the publisher.

All Scripture quotations in this publication are from the HOLY BIBLE,
NEW INTERNATIONAL VERSION NIV ® Copyright © 1973, 1978, 1984, 2011 by Biblica, Inc. ®
Used by permission. All rights reserved worldwide. The "NIV" and "New International Version"
are trademarks registered in the United States Patent and Trademark Office by Biblica, Inc. ®
Use of either trademark requires the permission of Biblica, Inc. ®

Scripture quotations marked by KJV are from the King James Version of the Bible.

Scripture quotations marked (NLT) are taken from the Holy Bible, New Living Translation,
copyright © 1996, 2004, 2007 by Tyndale House Foundation. Used by permission of Tyndale
House Publishers, Inc., Carol Stream, Illinois 60188.
All rights reserved.

Scripture quotations marked (ESV) are from The ESV® Bible (The Holy Bible,
English Standard Version®), copyright © 2001 by Crossway, a publishing ministry
of Good News Publishers. Used by permission. All rights reserved.

Printed in the United States of America

Library of Congress Cataloging-in-Publication Data

Second Edition 2017

1 2 3 4 5 6 7 8 9 10

DO NOT COPY

We worked really hard to make the Conquer Series, so please do not copy this book. We use the proceeds from the sale of our materials to create other materials that bring healing to the family. So, in essence, by purchasing this study guide you're investing in the healing of your wife and family. I think that's a great investment. Our mission is cut short when you photocopy our materials, plus it is illegal.

Additional study guides may be purchased at ConquerSeries.com. Group leaders may make a copy of the Conquer Group Guidelines to post at your group meetings, and may make additional copies of the Memo of Understanding.

Thank you for your support of KingdomWorks Studios and our mission.

Blessings,

Jeremy Wiles, CEO
KingdomWorks Studios

WHAT HAPPENS AFTER
THE CONQUER SERIES?

WARPATH

Warpath is a comprehensive, long-term course for men who have completed the Conquer Series. This powerful video series for men will equip you to live a life of sustained sexual integrity.

Hosted by Dr. Doug Weiss, psychologist, author and featured guest in the Conquer Series. Dr. Doug has trained thousands of men how to break free from sexual bondage. In Warpath he'll take you in-depth on the subjects presented in the Conquer Series and provide new tools and insights for building the DNA of a warrior.

WarpathSeries.com
Only available to watch online.

Acknowledgements

To Dr. Ted Roberts, Bryan Roberts, Harry Flanagan, Linda Dodge, Heather Kolb and Sauna Windsor: Your expertise, wisdom, and editorial contribution to this study guide have been indispensable. Dr. Ted, your leadership and example in this battle has been an inspiration to us, which has forever transformed us to be better servants of Christ.

To our family and friends who have been an inspiration and an encouragement to us: Thank you. Your prayers and support have helped us through the years, since we launched the Conquer Series.

Thank you to our precious prayer partners, Gwen, George, Julie, Sue, Frank, David, and Troy, who have been relentless in interceding for us and the men for whom we have created the Conquer Series. To Ronnie McElroy, thank you for faithfully staying in the journey with us. No one will fully understand the eternal value of your contributions to this project. We can't express enough of our gratitude to God for bringing each of you into our lives.

And to the loves-of-our-lives, Avalon and Landon: We fight this battle for you, so that your life's story may far exceed the chapters of our lives, as a new man and woman in Christ. We love you both so much!

To you, the reader, thank you for inviting us into your life. We pray that you will find the encouragement and tools you need from this curriculum to pursue real healing and freedom.

Dr. Ted Roberts

Host of the Conquer Series
Founder of Pure Desire Ministries

"I have been called to speak to the men of this generation and the next with a prophetic voice, calling them to walk in sexual integrity, with a strong passion for their divine destiny, by the grace of God and the power of the Holy Spirit. Challenging men to real manhood, not to remain in their present day spiritual passivity. Calling men to become hell's worst nightmare. Calling men to Conquer!"
– Dr. Ted Roberts

Dr. Ted Roberts is the host of the Conquer Series. This former U.S. Marine fighter pilot and Senior Pastor of East Hill Church in Oregon is the founder and leader of Pure Desire Ministries International, a ministry devoted to healing sexual addicts and their spouses, with a 90% success rate. A former sex addict himself, Dr. Roberts knows what it takes to conquer hell at close range. He has over thirty years of counseling experience helping men get free from sexual addiction and helping husbands and wives restore their marriages.

Jeremy & Tiana Wiles

Creators of the Conquer Series
Founders of KingdomWorks Studios

"There can never be healthy churches until we deal with sexual bondage in the Church. We cannot expect men in shackles to fight and lead, nor can we expect the lost and hurting to find healing in an ailing Church. When men unchain themselves from sexual sin, they can claim their roles as leaders and as men. On that day we will have strong marriages and families, and the Church will once again become the salt and light that it was meant to be in this increasingly dark world." - Jeremy & Tiana Wiles

Jeremy Wiles is an award-winning filmmaker with a vision to create benchmark Christian films rich in quality, content, and anointed by the Holy Spirit. Putting aside his first feature film Ark Hunter to produce the Conquer Series, Jeremy and his wife Tiana, dedicated two years of their lives to give the Church a proven battle plan that will change the game forever in the war against sexual bondage.

Contents

Getting Started

As a man, breaking free from sexual bondage will be one of the greatest challenges you will ever face in life, but it will also be one of the most rewarding. I want to encourage you to keep fighting because there is hope, regardless of how many times you've failed and how long you've struggled. The men who have chartered this rigorous road, and have prevailed, can assure you; you can be free and live the rest of your life with purity in this sex-saturated world. If you stay the course, you will discover what it truly means to be more than a conqueror through Christ.

As you embark on this journey, know that God loves you and will be with you throughout the process. His Word guarantees that He is able to do immeasurably more than all you ask or imagine, according to His power that is at work within you (Ephesians 3:20). God also says that His plans are to prosper you and not to harm you, to give you hope and a future (Jeremiah 29:11). So, take courage and comfort in these truths.

On that note, welcome to boot camp! Get ready to enter God's training ground for warriors; whenever you feel like quitting, remember that conquerors aren't born—they're made.

In Christ,

Jeremy & Tiana Wiles
Creators of the Conquer Series
Founders of KingdomWorks Studios

What Is The Conquer Series And Who Is It For?

The Conquer Series is for any man who has ever struggled. At some point, every man will be tempted to sin sexually. The difference between prevailing and failing comes down to having a battle plan in place. The Conquer Series video curriculum is comprehensive, training men to fight and win against sexual sin, teaching them how to live in sexual purity. This intensive discipleship course will take you out of your comfort zone, so expect to be challenged.

We advise parents and youth leaders to review the episodes and written materials before showing them to adolescents younger than 18 years old; you may find the content too mature for your child or youth group.

Defining Sexual Bondage

There is a disconnect among Christians when you mention sexual addiction, but addictions are real and Christians are not immune to this. Addictions are used as a coping mechanism to deal with life; they often represent symptoms of a much deeper issue seldom recognized by the person in addiction. We refer to addiction as "bondage" because we're ultimately dealing with strongholds. We alternately use the terms "bondage" and "addiction" throughout the Conquer Series.

In the context of this Series, sexual addiction refers to a broad spectrum of sexual sins, which a person cannot break. To name a few, if you cannot stop watching pornography, masturbating, having sexual fantasies, or engaging in sexual activities outside of the marriage covenant, then you are most likely in sexual bondage. You may experience periods of abstinence for weeks, months, or years, but you've never been able to stop your behavior. It is possible to love Christ with all your heart and be sexually addicted; it's not just a spiritual problem—it is also a brain problem.

The Sexual Addiction Screening Test (SAST) can help you determine if you have a sexual addiction by comparing your responses with people who have been diagnosed with sexual addiction. A score of six or higher indicates you likely have an addiction. The SAST is available in the appendix of this study guide and online through the Conquer Series website: **www.ConquerSeries.com/sast**

Using This Study Guide

This Study Guide, ideal for individual or small group study, is designed to help you make the most of the Conquer Series. The men who receive the maximum benefit are those who consistently apply what they are learning to their daily lives. It will take a conscious effort to break free from sexual bondage.

LESSON OVERVIEW
The Lesson Overview outlines the key topics and core concepts for the week. The Lesson Overview provides space for you to note specific insights as you watch each episode. The Summary Points from each episode are provided for you in this Study Guide.

DISCUSSION
This is where you wrestle with the concepts presented. As you gain a new understanding, you will be able to apply these practices to your life. Your learning will be greatly enhanced if this happens within a Conquer Group.

ACCOUNTABILITY
Following the discussion, group members will share their weekly struggles and progress, as well as keep each other accountable with their Commitment to Change throughout the week. This is a crucial part of the curriculum. Connecting with the members of your group on a regular basis will help you grow as a disciple of Jesus and accelerate your healing. Your accountability partners—the men in your group—will check-in with you and ask questions about how you are doing on your Commitment to Change.

7-DAY MISSION
This is your battle plan for the week. It may include questions to answer in this Study Guide and exercises to complete in your Conquer Series Journal. Throughout your healing process, journaling will provide a foundation for battling your addiction. Journaling will help you discover the nature of your sexual struggles and recognize patterns in your behavior. Over the next 10 weeks, you will journal on a daily basis. If you are new to journaling, cultivating this new discipline is essential to experiencing lifelong transformation.

Note: The 7-Day Mission provides a concise weekly battle plan built on the key concepts in the episode for you to work out in your Conquer Series Study Guide and Journal. Additional exercises mentioned in the Conquer Series are suggestions for you to add on your own.

Group Meeting Structure

Each week, allow up to two hours to view the episode, answer the group discussion questions, and complete the Commitment to Change. Make sure to bring your Conquer Series Journal to your Conquer Group meeting to review and complete your Commitment to Change.

If group members choose to watch the episode on their own before the meeting, each group member would need to purchase the Conquer Series. When choosing this option, your group may only need 60 to 90 minutes to complete the weekly group exercises.

The amount of time you spend in your group each week may vary based on the number of group members and the exercises within each lesson.

 The **(CLOCK)** icon, indicates the estimated time it takes to complete this part of the meeting.

 The **(GROUP)** icon indicates the section intended for group meetings.

FIRST MEETING
Your first Conquer Group meeting will include introductions; briefly getting to know the members of your group, and entering their contact information on page 8 of your Conquer Series Journal. As a group, you will review the Conquer Group guidelines, the purpose of accountability, as well as read and sign the Memo of Understanding and the Covenant to Contend.

ALL OTHER MEETINGS
After watching the Conquer Series episode, discuss the key topics and core concepts provided within the lesson. Share your experiences, struggles and progress based on your Commitment to Change and exercises from the previous lesson. Fill out your Commitment to Change for next week.

Watch the Conquer Series episode (approximately 30-45 minutes)
Discussion of this week's episode (approximately 30 minutes)
Debrief last week's 7-Day Mission and the accountability questions
(found in your Group Check-In.)
Fill out next week's Commitment to Change (approximately 30 minutes)

Conquer Group Guidelines

In order for all group members to have the best possible experience, we recommend the following guidelines.

Confidentiality is essential: What is said in the group is not shared outside of the group.

Speak only for yourself: Do not share information that is not yours to share.

Respect others: Let everyone find their own answers; do not give advice unless asked. Be present and involved during group meetings; no side conversations.

Limit personal sharing: Everyone in the group needs an opportunity to share.

Start and end on time: Use your time wisely; do not get stuck on rabbit-trails.

Come prepared: Review each lesson and take time to complete assignments.

Take responsibility: If you feel uncomfortable with anything happening during group or among group members, share your concern with the group or with the leader or co-leader.

How To Use The Guidelines

Agreement from the group is vital: Can everyone agree to the guidelines?

You may need to add one or two guidelines unique to your group members and their expectations for the group. For example, cell phone use during class. Discuss the issue, obtain agreement, and add the guideline.

Post the guidelines during group time so that group members are reminded of the agreed upon expectations for each other and the group.

Review the group guidelines when someone new joins the group.

Accountability

If you haven't already, we recommend that you join a Conquer Group. Asking others to support you and your personal goals—through accountability—is key to change. You cannot win this battle alone. Sexual bondage creates an intimacy disorder and strongholds produced by lies and denial. Secrets make you sick and hold you captive in your addiction, but healing starts when you realize that you are powerless on your own. With accountability, you'll discover the freedom in honesty, and willingly submit to the spiritual authority of your Christian brothers. We can help you find a Conquer Group or start one. For more information on joining an online or a local Conquer Group, visit ConquerSeries.com.

Typically, it takes 2 to 5 years for a man to break free from sexual bondage. Therefore, it is imperative that you continue in an accountability group. **There is no room for passivity or procrastination if you desire lifelong change.**

Once your group completes the Conquer Series, transition your current group into a more advanced accountability group and go much further in-depth with Warpath. This powerful video series for men will equip them for the long path ahead and provide them with the tools to live a life of sustained sexual integrity. Learn more at WarpathSeries.com.

How Does Accountability Work?

Each group will consist of five to eight members, including the group leader. Conquer Groups are designed to provide a safe environment where men can support one another through accountability, confess their struggles, and pray for each other, as the Bible commands us in James 5:16. This process allows the Holy Spirit to direct, heal, and restore the members of your Conquer Group; providing an opportunity for men to forge strong relationships built on trust, acceptance, and grace.

The leader and every member is required to sign a Memo of Understanding, which prohibits them from sharing anything disclosed in the group with others outside of the group. Confessing your struggles to one another can be daunting; but once you break through denial, you will feel relief. Remember, you're not fighting this battle alone, but with a combat team who has your back. This is your training ground for integrity and Christ-like manhood, so make the most of it.

Guidelines For Leaders

The primary role of the Conquer Group leader is to facilitate the meetings; acting as a moderator during the discussion and encouraging participation. The leader is responsible for providing a safe place where men are guaranteed trust, respect, and support. You are not expected to have counseling experience. To sign up as a group leader, visit our website at ConquerSeries.com.

Host your group meeting in a location where the conversation will remain private. If you meet in a home, create a casual setting. Before each meeting, make sure that the device you are viewing on is hooked up properly; ensure that you have good audio and visual quality. Since the lesson content may be intense and personal, we suggest that you have the lights dimmed or off while watching the episode. This will provide a more discreet and comfortable environment.

Before your first meeting, we recommend that you watch at least one episode to get a feel for the content. A Checklist for Group Leaders is provided in the appendix of this study guide and can be used to plan each meeting. Before starting Lesson 1, make sure that each group member signs the Memo of Understanding, which you can print from our website or copy from the study guide. Each member should sign and date the copy in their study guide, as well as an additional copy that you will keep on file. This is an agreement from each member stating that whatever is disclosed in the group stays in the group.

All the group members should read and sign the Covenant to Contend, which will remain in their study guide. For more information on facilitating a small group—and for inspiration—watch the Leader's training videos, get a copy of the Conquer Series Leader's Guide, and visit ConquerSeries.com for free resources for Conquer Group leaders. Remember to regularly pray for each member of your group. Allow for the Holy Spirit to do His part in your meetings, so that change and healing can take place.

Remember, this is not a 10-week journey, but an ongoing process. Based on the experience of group leaders who have successfully run the Conquer Series in their church, we recommend - once you complete the 10-week course - that you make the Conquer Series an ongoing ministry in your church, while simultaneously starting a Warpath group. The Warpath Series is a long-term study. It's important that you have an ongoing Conquer Group for men who need an introduction to the process. The Conquer Series is boot camp and perfect for those who are new to the process, while Warpath is advanced training for those who have already been introduced to the principles taught in the Conquer Series.

Guidelines For Group Members

Some of the discussion and accountability questions may be unnerving, but do your best to participate. This is bootcamp. You are expected to do your part. Your participation, or lack of it, will affect the members of your group, as well as your own learning and recovery process. Through your openness, you will encourage others to do the same, creating an atmosphere of trust, healing, and brotherly love. When you are honest about your struggles, you inspire and challenge others to do the same.

While watching the Conquer Series, and during discussion, take good notes so that you can implement what you are learning. Complete the exercises in your Conquer Series Journal on a daily basis. When you pray and meditate on God's Word, remember that God is with you; His Holy Spirit will guide and strengthen you throughout this healing process.

Memo Of Understanding

Conquer Group Participants: Please read and sign this Memo of Understanding, indicating that you have read and understood the purpose and parameters of Conquer Groups and the moral and ethical obligations of leaders.

I understand that every attempt will be made to guard my anonymity and confidentiality in this group, but that anonymity and confidentiality cannot be absolutely guaranteed in a group setting.

- I realize that the group coordinator or leader cannot control the actions of others in the group.
- I realize that confidentiality is sometimes broken accidentally and without malice.

I understand that the group coordinator or leader is morally and ethically obligated to discuss with me any of the following behaviors, and that this may lead to the breaking of confidentiality and/or possibly intervention:

- I communicate anything that may be interpreted as a threat to self-inflict physical harm.
- I communicate an intention to harm another person.
- I reveal ongoing sexual or physical abuse.
- I exhibit an impaired mental state.

I understand that the Conquer Group coordinator or leader may be a mandatory reporter to authorities of sexual conduct that includes minor children, the elderly or the disabled.

I have been advised that the consequences for communicating the above types of information may include reports to the proper authorities: the police, suicide units or children's protective agencies, as well as potential victims.

I further acknowledge that if I am on probation and/or parole and I engage in wrongful behavior in violation of my parole/probation, part of my healing/recovery may include notifying appropriate authorities.

I understand that this is a Christ-centered group that integrates recovery tools with the Bible and prayer, and that all members may not be of a particular church background. I realize that the Bible may be discussed more (or less) than the way that I would like it to be.

I understand that this is a support group and not a therapy group and that the coordinator/leader may be qualified by "life experience" and not by professional training as a therapist or counselor. The coordinator/leader is a volunteer, whose role is mainly to host the Conquer Series and create a climate where healing may occur, to support my work toward recovery, and to share my own experience, strength and hope.

I hereby pledge that anything discussed in my Conquer Group, among group members and the group leader, will remain confidential. I pledge not to share any personal information to anyone outside of the group, unless any of the above criminal activities is involved.

Name [please print]

_____

Signature: _____   Date: _____

WITNESS

Conquer Group Leader Name: _____

Conquer Group Leader Signature : _____

Covenant To Contend

There is a battle going on within me. As much as it pains me to admit it, that battlefield is my sexuality. I realize that the outcome of this battle not only holds my life in its hands, but the lives of those I love and care for. I now choose to participate in the battle for godly character and integrity, not only for my soul, but also for my family, friends, brothers and sisters in Christ and, above all else, Almighty God.

I am beginning to understand I cannot win this battle by myself. I am coming to see the biblical truth that "We are members of one another." Therefore, I surrender to His wisdom, turn to the leadership of the Church, and submit myself to the process of the renewing of my mind.

THINGS I CAN DO
- Attend a small group weekly.
- God's values supersede mine; therefore, I will contend to live life on His terms instead of mine or of the culture around me.
- Pay close attention to what I look at; what I listen to; what I set my mind on.
- Take responsibility for my thoughts and actions.
- Verbally describe my feelings.
- Make contact with all my Conquer Group members between our weekly group meetings.

I CAN ACCEPT
- Healing is a miraculous process over time.
- Healing requires feeling the pain and learning from it.
- I am very capable of retreating back into the addictive lifestyle.
- A relapse does not stop the healing process, but it will have consequences.
- I have become skilled at lying to others and myself.
- I do not really live in isolation; my choices do affect others.
- My secrecy keeps me in bondage to my sin.

I WILL COMMIT TO
- A willingness to change—and following through with my plans.
- Total confidentiality! I discuss only my experiences outside the group.
- Rigorous honesty with God, my Conquer Group, myself, and eventually to my friends and family.
- Building my knowledge base (books, CDs, videos, and seminars).
- Reading Scripture, praying and a biblical standard of sexual purity in my life.
- A goal of moving toward sobriety that is living God's way.

Signature: _____   Date: _____

Witnessed by : _____

Covenant to Contend © 2009 Pure Desire Ministries International

Understanding
the Battlefield

Understanding The Battlefield
Week 1, Episode 1

This lesson is based on Episode 1 of the Conquer Series. Read this introduction before watching Episode 1 and attending your Conquer Group.

"Do not be afraid, you worm Jacob, little Israel, do not fear, for I myself will help you," declares the Lord, your Redeemer, the Holy One of Israel. "See, I will make you into a threshing sledge, new and sharp, with many teeth. You will thresh the mountains and crush them, and reduce the hills to chaff. **– Isaiah 41:14–15**

Do we really get this? Do we truly understand that the God of the universe calls mortal men like us to be a weapon of war in His hands? It is human nature to stay within our comfort zone, which is why the notion of waging war is not our natural predisposition. Whether you like it or not, the moment you gave your life to Christ you were called to fight against hell. But before you can be a threat to the enemy, a conqueror must be tested through fire and shaped into the image of God's Son, Jesus Christ.

Sexual bondage is one of Satan's master plans against men as it doesn't just prevent us from growing into the image of Christ, but distorts His very image in us and leaves us ineffective. Countless men in sexual bondage have tried fighting this battle; instead of finding victory, they are beaten down by their sin, eventually losing their identity in Christ. When a man becomes disoriented in battle, he loses his ability to accomplish his mission.

The first thing you need to understand is the battlefield. In this lesson you will learn about the scope of the war, the enemy's strategies and weapons, where the battle takes place, and where you've gone wrong in your fight against sexual sin. This week you will be introduced to the core principles of conquering sexual bondage, which are necessary for accomplishing your mission. Through spiritual and practical tools, you will begin the process of healing and moving toward freedom. This is a week where you must leave your comfort zone and be prepared to do anything God wants you to do to break free.

Prayer for Change

Heavenly Father, thank You for the cross. I come to You with brokenness, asking You to forgive me, restore me, and show me how to break my chains so I can truly live for You and make my life count. I have made a decision to fight and win this battle once and for all. I commit these next few weeks to You. By Your power I can be healed, I can be free, and I can become a conqueror. I ask this in Jesus' name, amen.

EPISODE 1 – Lesson Overview

The four principles you must understand to accomplish your mission:

1. The weapons of the enemy.
2. The strategy of the enemy.
3. The weapons of God.
4. God's battle plan for purity.

Facts and figures: A study of over 3000 data points discovered that 60–70 percent of men, 50–58 percent of pastors, and 20–30 percent of women in evangelical churches are sexually addicted.

How do we define sexual addiction? "When you cannot stop your behavior; when you're spending more time and money than you thought you would; when you've been caught or had consequences but continue anyway; when you've made promises to quit and can't fulfill those promises to yourself, God, your family, and your wife, you most likely have an addiction."
—Dr. Doug Weiss

Porn is a problem at any dose, and it doesn't need to be utilized at any dose. It's like I wouldn't tell people: "Well, as long as you're not addicted to cocaine, cocaine is fine." No, it's not!

— Dr. Tim Jennings, M.D. FAPA

NOTES:

_____

_____

_____

_____

_____

The Kinsey factor: According to Dr. Judith Reisman, the publishing of the Kinsey Reports was a turning point in history which opened the door to sexual immorality in America. The Kinsey Reports were based on fraudulent data submitted by rapists, pedophiles, and prison inmates who systematically molested and raped hundreds of children for "scientific" information. They recorded their "experiments" with a ledger and a stopwatch.

The information compiled in the Kinsey Reports sought to change our opinions about sexuality and to convince the public that we are sexual from birth. Ultimately, our perspective on our sexuality did change, which ignited the sexual revolution. Over time, penalties for sexual crimes were lessened and pornography and abortion were legalized. America now stands as the number one exporter of pornography to the rest of the world.

God's original plan for sex was to reveal His image in the covenant relationship between a husband and wife. Your body is the temple of the Holy Spirit; therefore, any sexual activity or behavior outside of marriage, whether you're single or married, is sin. Read "The Bible and Sexual Sin" in the appendix of this study guide.

> *God created our sexuality to be beautiful... To be something that brings great joy, and yet man, in the Fall, has perverted that. Ever since that's been perverted it's been a battle of whether it is something of beauty or something that degrades people. Something that brings joy or something that brings bondage.*
>
> **— Paul Cole, Christian Men's Network**

NOTES:

_____

_____

_____

The Noose of Bondage: Understanding the noose of bondage is key to your freedom. The noose is composed of:

1. The root: Wounds
2. The mindset: Having a shame perspective of oneself
3. The lifestyle: Binge-purge cycle
4. The cloak: Denial, delusion, and blame

The importance of processing the wound: King David was referred to as a "HaKatan," a worthless one, by his father. This sense of worthlessness worked its way down into David's soul. Like David, many successful men become entangled in sexual sin because they have failed to process their wounds. The majority of sex addicts in church come from rigid, disengaged religious homes dominated by rules and lacking in relationship. It is important to discover the root—the wounds in our lives—in order to find true healing and freedom. The place where you were wounded is where the enemy has inserted a lie about you. However, sexual addiction isn't always caused by wounds, as there are men who become addicted simply by watching pornography; once they are hooked, they learn to deal with life by resorting to pornography, sex, and masturbation, to name a few. Sexually acting out becomes a coping mechanism. The majority of men trapped in sexual bondage have wounds from their past.

A secret idol: Finding satisfaction in sexuality, rather than in God, is a form of idol worship because it replaces our reverence and need for God.

What a man loves, he protects. — **Dr. Doug Weiss**

NOTES:

_____

_____

_____

_____

_____

SUMMARY POINTS
- Seventy percent of Christian men struggling with sexual bondage come from homes where rules override relationship.[1]
- Sexual sin promises to serve and please, but only desires to dominate and destroy.
- In most cases, wounds are the root of sexual bondage.

[1] Roberts, T. (2009). Seven Pillars of Freedom Workbook. Gresham, OR: Pure Desire Ministries International.

Discussion

Watch Episode 1 of the Conquer Series before answering the following questions:

1. What one idea or fact about addiction stands out to you that you learned from in this lesson?

_____

_____

2. What did you learn about the process involved in overcoming and healing from addiction?

_____

_____

3. What is significant about processing the wound? What feelings come to mind when you think about processing your wounds?

_____

_____

Accountability

1. What do you expect from being part of a Conquer Group?

_____

_____

2. What are you struggling with today and how is it affecting the people you love?

_____

_____

3. Your 7-Day Mission this week includes cleaning your house of all porn and completing a chart to identify all electronic devices that can access porn. Go to the 7-Day Mission section in this chapter (step 3) and spend 5 to 10 minutes filling in the chart during your Conquer Group meeting. Discuss with your group the areas you plan to protect this week and the people you must talk to regarding these changes.

Your 7-Day Mission – Week 1

1. JOIN A CONQUER GROUP

If you haven't already, join a Conquer Group—an accountability group—and sign the Covenant to Contend together. It will take a strong group of guys to help you fulfill the commitment you made to walk in integrity and purity. To find a Conquer Group in your area or join an online group, register at ConquerSeries.com (your information will remain confidential). Read and sign the Memo of Understanding during your first Conquer Group meeting.

2. TAKE THE SAST

As a group, make a commitment to complete the SAST this week. Please take the test before the next group meeting. You can take the test online at **ConquerSeries.com/sast,** or complete the SAST in the appendix of this study guide. Remember, if you score six or more in the first 20 items, you meet the clinical definition of a sex addict. However, it is not your identity; it will help you define what the battlefield will look like for you.

3. CLEAN YOUR HOUSE OF ALL PORN AND PROTECT YOUR DEVICES

Any and all movies, books, magazines, and apps that are pornographic in nature MUST GO! You cannot win this battle if you are not willing to let go of the devices that the enemy uses to ensnare you.

Protecting your devices includes every piece of electronic equipment: computers, smart phones, iPads and gaming systems. Invest in an accountability software program for all of your devices. Use the following table to list all your devices, the necessary level of protection, people you need to talk to regarding these changes, and check it off your list when completed. Use this table as a point of reference during your group discussion this week.

Installing filters and blocking controls are helpful, but you need an accountability reporting system that sends a report to a member of your Conquer Group, alerting them of your Internet use. It is amazing how quickly men learn self-discipline when they experience full accountability with the men in their group.

These changes are significant and may affect others in your life, but your healing depends on it. You may need to talk with your family, boss, coworkers, or roommates. Your family needs to know what changes you are making regarding the connections in the house, but we do not recommend that you ask them for accountability.

CONNECTION	PROTECTION	PEOPLE I NEED TO TALK TO	√ WHEN COMPLETED
Laptop **Home computer**	Which accountability software will you use?	**Wife and kids:** I am making these changes... **Group member:** Will you read my accountability reports and keep me accountable?	
Work computer	Which accountability software will you use?	**Supervisor:** Can I use this software at work? **Group member:** Will you read my accountability reports and keep me accountable?	
Cable TV	Set parental controls for inappropriate content.	**Wife and kids:** I am making these changes so that inappropriate shows cannot be viewed in our house.	
Smartphone **Smartwatch** **Tablet**	Which accountability software will you use?	**Wife and kids:** I am making these changes... **Group member:** Will you read my accountability reports and keep me accountable?	

That is the purpose of your Conquer Group. The guys in your group should be calling each week to ask how you are doing with your Internet usage or when they receive an accountability report from your Internet filtering and online accountability provider when they have questions.

4. CALL EACH MEMBER IN YOUR CONQUER GROUP

Commit to calling <u>all</u> the men in your Conquer Group each week. Ask them how they are doing on their 7-Day Mission and to let them know your progress as well. Your Conquer Series Journal not only provides a page for you to list all the members in your group and their contact information, but a weekly Call Schedule to organize who and when to contact throughout the week. Questions to ask your group members are included with the weekly Call Schedule.

5. JOURNAL YOUR BATTLES

True healing starts by learning to journal your battles. Each day, through the use of your Conquer Series Journal, you will begin to discover patterns in your behavior; identifying your urges, triggers and fantasies. As you become more aware and write about your behaviors, you will recognize what keeps you trapped in the cycle of addiction, as well as how to break that cycle and change direction. Journaling your battles on a daily basis will help you change and grow, launching you on your journey toward lasting health and freedom.

7-Day Mission Checklist – Week 1

Note: *The 7-Day Mission provides a concise weekly battle plan built on the key concepts in the episode for you to work out in your Conquer Series Study Guide and Journal. Additional exercises mentioned in the Conquer Series are suggestions for you to add on your own.*

☐ Joined a Conquer Group

☐ Took the Sexual Addiction Screening Test (SAST): ConquerSeries.com/sast

☐ Cleaned my house of all porn and installed accountability software
on all my Internet devices

☐ Called all the men in my Conquer Group this week

☐ Daily journaled my battles in my Conquer Series Journal

The Mission

The Mission

 This lesson is based on Episode 2 of the Conquer Series. Read this introduction before watching Episode 2 and attending your Conquer Group.

 Therefore, since we are surrounded by such a great cloud of witnesses, let us throw off everything that hinders and the sin that so easily entangles. And let us run with perseverance the race marked out for us, fixing our eyes on Jesus, the pioneer and perfecter of faith... – Hebrews 12:1-2

Last week, we looked at the battlefield and how Satan uses our sexual sin against us. He is a master-manipulator; using our area of weakness as a weapon against us, destroying our relationship with God and others. It is time to learn how to fight back.

It starts by examining the four components of the Noose of Sexual Bondage and learning how to sever the strands that have you ensnared. So many men have believed the lie that trying harder will break the chains of addiction; but trying harder won't work. Sexual addiction is the result of a wounded heart, a wound that many men have carried with them since childhood—a wound that only the Spirit of God can heal.

Shame and guilt play a significant role in the addiction process, not only keeping us trapped in our addiction, but pulling us farther from relationships, fueling our desire for isolation. Accountability is key. You will not win this battle alone. Through the men who walk beside you— the men who are in the trenches, fighting for sexual purity—you will be strengthened. Together, you will experience healing and freedom like never before.

This week, your mission will include implementing the spiritual and practical tools introduced in this lesson. Your ability to focus on your healing will be reinforced by the members of your Conquer Group, by trying smarter - not harder.

Prayer for Change

 Father in Heaven, thank you for the plan that You have for my life. Although I may not see the full-scope of what You are going to accomplish in me, help me to keep my eyes on You. Thank You for the men You have brought to my group, who will walk with me through this battle. Help me to trust You and fully commit to this process. I want to change and grow in You. In Jesus' name, amen.

EPISODE 2 – Lesson Overview

Components of the Noose: It isn't just one thing—one strand of the noose—that keeps men enslaved, held captive in sexual bondage. The four strands of the noose work together, strengthening their grasp:

1. The root of bondage, which are past wounds and trauma.
2. The mindset of shame or having a shame perspective: "Something is wrong with me."
3. The lifestyle of bondage: engaging in a binge-purge cycle.
4. The cloak of denial: the justification of our choices.

Shame perspective: Many men cannot understand why they struggle to beat sexual bondage. Despite trying harder, the problem is not in willpower; they're dealing with a wounded heart. They're carrying shame within their soul. Shame is different than guilt. To use a football analogy: Guilt—you stepped out of bounds. Shame—you can't get the ball in the end zone no matter what you do; you're convinced there's something wrong with you.

NOTES:

_____

_____

_____

_____

_____

_____

_____

_____

_____

_____

_____

_____

_____

_____

That [pornography and other sexual sins] can get into a man's heart to the place where it replaces God...It becomes an idol. And how do you know it's an idol? When you're in pain, you go to your idol. When you're in need, you go to your idol. When you're hurt, you go to your idol. When you want to celebrate, you go to your idol.
— Dr. Doug Weiss

Not just a moral problem: Most Christian men in sexual bondage love God with all their heart. They pray and read their Bible daily, but can't stop their behavior. We have to realize that sexual bondage isn't mainly a moral problem, but a brain problem. Addiction influences the brain's neurochemicals, changing the structure of the brain. Understanding the problem is the first step to freedom. It typically takes 2 to 5 years to break free from sexual-and porn addiction. This process requires the renewing of the mind through Christ.

The three keys to freedom:

1. Break denial structures.
2. Understand the bondage cycle.
3. Access the deep wound.

NOTES:

_____

_____

_____

_____

_____

_____

_____

_____

_____

Sexual bondage is not about sex, it's about how you've learned to medicate the pain in your life. Once you start facing this, your pain level is actually going to go up. Because you've been medicating that pain for so long, you'll have to put your big boy pants on and you'll have to face the pain. This is going to challenge you as a man more than anything you have ever done in your life.
                                                                    — **Dr. Ted Roberts**

Tools to Conquer: A fighting chance against the enemy.

It is so important to understand that the battle is in your brain. Therefore, there are three things that must take place for you to have a fighting chance against the enemy.

1. Become aware of the what, when, where, why and how of your acting out.
2. Become accountable to yourself and others.
3. Pay it forward by helping other men find freedom.

NOTES:

_____

_____

_____

_____

_____

_____

_____

_____

_____

_____

_____

_____

_____

_____

SUMMARY POINTS

- Sexual bondage is not about sex, but how you have learned to medicate the pain and stress in your life.
- Men usually find sobriety within 90 days, but true transformation requires 2-5 years of ongoing commitment to this process with a miracle every day.

Trying harder doesn't work: It's crucial to understand that your integrity and your legacy are determined by your sexual integrity. The first step is realizing that trying harder doesn't work—you need to learn how to fight. You need to understand the battle; know your mission and learn to apply God's weapons and strategies to your battle.

Discussion

Watch Episode 2 of the Conquer Series before answering the following questions:

1. Why doesn't trying harder work when it comes to sexual bondage?

_____

_____

2. Why can't you win this battle alone?

_____

_____

3. Dr. Doug Weiss says, "What a man loves, he protects." What do you love?

_____

_____

4. Considering the Noose of Sexual Bondage, which strand of the noose has the strongest grasp in your life?

_____

_____

Accountability

Note: *If there are new members in the group, have them read and sign the Memo of Understanding and Covenant to Contend before proceeding with this section.*

Last week's 7-Day Mission

1. Did you join a Conquer Group?

_____

_____

2. What did you score on the SAST?

_____

_____

3. Housecleaning: On a scale of 0 (no porn) to 10 (a lot of porn), what is your progress on ridding your house of all porn?

0	1	2	3	4	5	6	7	8	9	10

porn-free house   a lot of porn

Placing accountability software on all your devices: look at the connection and protection-plan table you filled out last week. How much did you accomplish? Name the device, protection, and people you talked with.

4. What was your experience with calling all the men in your Conquer Group?

_____

_____

5. Journaling your battles: how did it go? Have you established a time and place to do your daily journaling? As you mentally review your week and your Journal Exercise, what did you battle with most? Did you discover any patterns?

_____

_____

Your 7-Day Mission – Week 2

1. COMMITMENT TO CHANGE

This week, you will continue developing accountability through your Commitment to Change. It is only through recognizing your harmful behaviors, and allowing others to keep you accountable, that you will experience lifelong healing. In your Conquer Series Journal, answer the questions regarding your Commitment to Change. This is something you will do every week at the end of your Conquer Group meeting.

2. CALL EVERY MEMBER IN YOUR CONQUER GROUP

Using the Call Schedule in your Conquer Series Journal, call every member in your Conquer Group this week. Connecting with the men in your group will help break isolation, reinforcing accountability and unity within the group. You may feel awkward at first, but use the Commitment to Change to guide the conversation. Ask them how they are doing on their Commitment to Change and report to them how you are doing.

3. PREPARE FOR THE BATTLE EACH NIGHT

It is common for men who struggle with pornography and sexual addiction to masturbate before they go to sleep at night or when they wake up in the morning. Therefore, if you want to break the Noose of Sexual Bondage, you must prepare for battle each night. Here's what this looks like:

- Turn off all electronic devices 30 minutes before you go to sleep.
- Spend 10 minutes practicing deep diaphragmic breathing. This calms your limbic system, or what Scripture refers to as your heart.
- Spend 20 minutes doing something edifying in the Holy Spirit—meditating on Scripture and allowing the Holy Spirit into your heart each night.

According to neuroscience, 10 percent of your brain works when you're awake, and 90 percent works when you're not. Your brain cleans itself out when you sleep - pruning old neural connections that aren't being used. So if you're not dabbling with porn, your brain will start to prune the synapses associated with porn viewing. Therefore, this exercise of preparing for the battle each night - meditating on Scripture before bed - is crucial. Why? Because God's Word has the power to physically restructure our brain. Most of the conscious decisions we make will continue to operate on an unconscious level - while we're sleeping.

Developing this discipline will help you start winning the battle each night, allowing you to dream of who God has called you to be.

7-Day Mission Checklist – Week 2

Note: *The 7-Day Mission provides a concise weekly battle plan built on the key concepts in the episode for you to work out in your Conquer Series Study Guide and Journal. Additional exercises mentioned in the Conquer Series are suggestions for you to add on your own.*

☐ Filled out the Commitment to Change in my Conquer Series Journal

☐ Called each member in my Conquer Group

☐ Prepared for battle each night

The Battle of
the Brain

03

The Battle of the Brain

Week 3, Episode 3

 This lesson is based on Episode 3 of the Conquer Series. Read this introduction before watching Episode 3 and attending your Conquer Group.

 So I find this law at work: Although I want to do good, evil is right there with me. For in my inner being I delight in God's law; but I see another law at work in me, waging war against the law of my mind and making me a prisoner of the law of sin at work within me. What a wretched man I am! Who will rescue me from this body that is subject to death? Thanks be to God, who delivers me through Jesus Christ our Lord!
– Romans 7:21-25

Is it possible for a man to love Christ with all his heart and yet struggle with sexual sin? The Apostle Paul understood the dichotomy between the flesh and the spirit. The former wants to serve the flesh, while the latter wants to serve Christ.

Unfortunately, many spiritual leaders, with the best intentions, have mistakenly treated sexual bondage as a moral problem. Men have been told that if they pray harder, read their Bible more, act more Christ-like—if they try harder—they would find healing. Some men have even had their pastors lay hands on them and the spiritual oppression may lift for awhile; but because they have not been given a process for renewing their mind, they find themselves falling back into the same old habit.

Failure to know where the battle takes place is detrimental because you'll keep trying to fix the problem with the wrong solution, often making matters worse. The battle for sexual purity is a battle of the mind; one that takes place in your brain. It is possible for a man to genuinely love Christ, but fail to stop his addiction on his own.

Knowing how God designed your brain will change the way you approach your struggle with sexual bondage. In this lesson, we will explore the science behind sexual bondage and discover the role of neuroplasticity: the brain's ability to adapt and reorganize throughout life. You will be given practical approaches on how to retrain your brain. The goal is to renew your mind and be transformed into the image of Christ.

Prayer for Change

 Father God, show me how to renew my mind, which has been corrupted by my sin. I humble myself before You and ask that You listen to my desperate cry for change. My eyes are on Your Son, Jesus Christ. Give me the patience to persevere and help me cooperate with the Holy Spirit this week. In Jesus' name, amen.

EPISODE 3 – Lesson Overview

Where the battle takes place: In the New Testament, the word "warfare" appears five times in the exact same context. It always refers to the battle of the mind. See 2 Corinthians 10:3-5, James 4:1, and James 1:14.

Sinning against your body: In 1 Corinthians 6:18, Paul explains that sexual sins are not like any other type of sin. When you sexually sin, you sin against your own body. Based on advances in the field of neuroscience, we now know that when you have a sexual release, your brain is flooded with neurochemicals that are as strong as drugs. So when you are sexually acting out, you are restructuring your brain and setting yourself up for sexual bondage.

James 1:14–15 says, "...but each person is tempted when they are dragged away by their own evil desire and enticed. Then, after desire has conceived, it gives birth to sin; and sin, when it is full-grown, gives birth to death." The word "entice" refers to a baited hook. When desire is conceived it gives birth to sin. In the context of sexual bondage, sexually acting out becomes a predetermined, pre-programmed pattern in your soul. James concludes by saying: "And sin, when it's fully-grown, gives birth to death." A man in sexual bondage is violating his core beliefs, which results in spiritual death, the death of his relationships, his dreams, and sometimes his body.

Whatever attracts and holds your attention will
eventually control the direction of your life. — **Paul Cole**

NOTES:

_____

_____

_____

_____

_____

_____

_____

SUMMARY POINTS

- Sexual sin is against your own body because it changes the physical composition of the brain.
- The war is waged in the brain.
- Sexual bondage starts as a moral issue that quickly develops into a brain problem.
- Understanding how God designed the brain is a key to breaking free from sexual bondage and staying pure.

The brain typically weighs three pounds. It makes up 2% of your body mass but uses 20% of your energy. It is composed of over 100 billion neurons. There are more neural connections in the brain than there are stars in our Milky Way galaxy. Recently, science has confirmed that the brain is pliable until death. New neural connections are constantly being made.[1]

NOTES:

_____

_____

_____

_____

_____

_____

_____

_____

_____

_____

SUMMARY POINTS

- Neurons that fire together, wire together.
- Each time you repeat a thought or an action, you create neurological pathways in the brain, causing these patterns of thought to become subconscious and programmed in your mind.
- These neurological pathways program your thought life and actions, so that they become second nature.

[1] Roberts, T. (2009). Seven Pillars of Freedom Workbook. Gresham, OR: Pure Desire Ministries International.

The analytic brain vs. the emotional brain: The prefrontal cortex is where higher reasoning takes place. It is our brain's chief commander and impulse control center. We make moral and ethical decisions with our prefrontal cortex. It isn't fully developed until the age of twenty-five. The limbic system is our survival system and operates on impulse and on a subconscious level. It overpowers the prefrontal cortex during times of fight or flight. The limbic system is the part of the brain where sexual bondage takes place. This is our emotional brain, where emotional memories are stored. So, what happens during times of stress or anger in a sexual addict's brain? The limbic system will overpower the prefrontal cortex.

Your internal pharmacy: The brain produces neurochemicals and hormones that create pleasure, help you bond with others, and forget pain, among other things. These neurochemicals flood the brain during sexual release. God designed us to produce these neurochemicals, but when used outside of His will, they become damaging to us.

Dopamine is a neurotransmitter that helps control the brain's reward and pleasure centers. Dopamine also helps regulate emotional responses, enabling us to identify rewards and take action toward them. In sexual addiction, dopamine surges into the pleasure circuits, as drugs do, and will cause alteration in gene expression in certain areas of the brain, damaging those areas.

NOTES:

_____

_____

_____

_____

_____

_____

_____

_____

_____

_____

_____

_____

_____

Tools to Conquer: The FASTER Scale.

If we're not present and not aware of how we feel throughout the day, we will find ourselves on the verge of relapse and won't know how we got there. When we learn to live in the present, we will be able to predict a relapse weeks before it happens. The FASTER Scale, developed by Michael Dye, is a powerful tool that will help you identify the behaviors, attitudes and feelings associated with the circumstances that lead to relapse.[2]

Every letter in the word "FASTER" indicates a level of behaviors, attitudes and feelings that often cover or mask our true emotion of pain and fear. The scale depicts how easily our behaviors progress, on a slippery-slope, ending in relapse. Whether the provocation is neurological or environmental, the pattern of movement toward relapse will become more obvious over time. Developing an awareness of our unique behaviors and patterns will help us avoid relapse, implement an intervention strategy, and maintain restoration.

We start off in Restoration: if you're here, that's great! It means you are accepting life on God's terms with trust, vulnerability and gratitude. This is where we want to live. This is the goal.

Forgetting priorities: Here is where we start to believe that our present circumstances define our life and we begin to move away from trusting God. We fall back into denial, we avoid and blame others, and our priorities start to change. This can lead to:

Anxiety: This is where we become fearful and anxious; our emotions begin to control us. Notice how the further you slide down the FASTER Scale, the more you are limbically or emotionally reactive? This can lead to:

Speeding up: Now you're trying to outrun anxiety, where depression and feelings of inadequacy and worthlessness come to the surface. This can lead to:

Ticked off: You're getting an adrenaline high from anger and aggressive behaviors. This can lead to:

Exhausted: The adrenaline is wearing off and you're on the brink of relapse. You are running out of physical or emotional energy. This can lead to:

Relapse: You act out—You've returned to the place you swore to never return.

---

[2] Dye, M. (2012). The Genesis Process: for change groups book 1 and 2 individual Workbook (4th ed.). Michael Dye.

Each time you relapse, you will have gone through the entire FASTER Scale. Using this tool on a daily basis will help you identify your feelings, based on your behaviors and attitudes, and make the appropriate changes to step-off the FASTER Scale and avoid relapse. Remember, the only way we can change our behavior is to recognize it, discover where it comes from, and make the necessary transitions to change direction.

Utilizing this tool takes time and intention. The Conquer Series Journal includes a daily FASTER Scale to help begin the process of renewing the mind. If you have not done so, order the Conquer Series Journal today. Throughout the remainder of this series, your 7-Day Mission will include the daily use of the FASTER Scale, which is explained in greater detail in the Conquer Series Journal.

Discussion

Watch Episode 3 of the Conquer Series before answering the following questions:

1. Run from sexual sin! No other sin so clearly affects the body as this one does. For sexual immorality is a sin against your own body. Don't you realize that your body is the temple of the Holy Spirit, who lives in you and was given to you by God? You do not belong to yourself, for God bought you with a high price. So you must honor God with your body. (1 Corinthians 6:18–20 NLT)

What facts can you learn about sexual sin from Paul's words to the Corinthian Christians?

_____

_____

What is your response to 1 Corinthians 6:18–20?

_____

_____

2. Paul Cole said, "Whatever attracts and holds your attention will eventually control the direction of your life." What is one thing in your life that is currently attracting and holding your attention?

_____

_____

3. Tell about a time when your limbic brain (emotional brain) overpowered your prefrontal cortex (moral brain)?

_____

_____

4. What are your thoughts and/or feelings regarding the FASTER Scale and implementing this tool on a daily basis?

_____

_____

Accountability

Note: *If there are any new members in the group, have them read and sign the Memo of Understanding and Covenant to Contend before proceeding with this part.*

Last week's 7-Day Mission

1. How successful were you on your Commitment to Change from last week?

_____

_____

2. Were you able to connect with every member in your Conquer Group?

_____

_____

3. How did you do with preparing for battle each night? What aspect was most challenging for you?

_____

_____

Your 7-Day Mission – Week 3

1. THE FASTER SCALE

The FASTER Scale can help you identify when you're on the verge of a relapse (acting out). Whenever you start sliding down the scale, immediately call at least one man in your Conquer Group. When you recognize behaviors that propel you toward relapse, try to identify the issues and work with the members of your group to get back to restoration. Remember, you don't have to work back through the preceding steps; simply step off the FASTER Scale and return to restoration.

If you started working in your Conquer Series Journal in week 1, you are already familiar with the FASTER Scale. Using this tool on a daily basis is critical for renewing the mind and finding lifelong healing.

2. JOURNAL YOUR BATTLES

Many men struggle with the journaling process, but hopefully you are becoming more comfortable with the process. Journaling can be very cathartic. Make sure to set aside quiet, uninterrupted time to journal throughout the week. Write about the urges and thoughts you're battling this week. Be prepared to share your struggles when you call the members of your Conquer Group this week.

3. CALL EACH MEMBER IN YOUR CONQUER GROUP

One of the core components of addictive behavior is isolation. The members of your Conquer Group are there to encourage and support you, regardless of what you may be going through. In the same way, you are to be there for them. Use the Call Schedule in your Conquer Series Journal to keep track of all the contacts you make this week.

4. PREPARE FOR BATTLE EACH NIGHT

Every night, practice the following disciplines:

- Turn off all electronic devices 30 minutes before you go to sleep.
- Spend 10 minutes practicing deep diaphragmic breathing.
  This calms your limbic system, or what Scripture refers to as your heart.
- Spend 20 minutes doing something edifying in the Holy Spirit—meditating on Scripture and allowing the Holy Spirit into your heart each night.

7-Day Mission Checklist – Week 3

Note: *The 7-Day Mission provides a concise weekly battle plan built on the key concepts in the episode for you to work out in your Conquer Series Study Guide and Journal. Additional exercises mentioned in the Conquer Series are suggestions for you to add on your own.*

☐ Used the FASTER Scale daily in my Conquer Series Journal

☐ Journaled my battles throughout the week

☐ Called each member in my Conquer Group

☐ Prepared for battle each night

Renewing
the Mind

04

Renewing the Mind
Week 4, Episode 4

This lesson is based on Episode 4 of the Conquer. Read this introduction before watching Episode 4 and attending your Conquer Group.

But that is not the way you learned Christ!—assuming that you have heard about him and were taught in him, as the truth is in Jesus, to put off your old self, which belongs to your former manner of life and is corrupt through deceitful desires, and to be renewed in the spirit of your minds, and to put on the new self, created after the likeness of God in true righteousness and holiness. – Ephesians 4:20-24 (ESV)

How is it that our brain, approximately three pounds of grey matter, is where bondage takes place? As previously mentioned, sexual addiction is not mainly a moral problem but a brain problem.

Satan will use anything he can to lure you away from your relationship with God and others. His plan is to use an imitation of sexual intimacy—pornography, fantasy, masturbation, affairs—to hold you captive and eventually destroy you. This is why it is so important that you understand the neurochemicals involved in sexual addiction and the role they play in the addictive process.

Within the context of marriage, God intended for a husband and wife to become "one flesh" when their brain releases bonding hormones during sexual intimacy. However, when a man is watching porn, these same bonding hormones are released causing him to bond with the image. This is what keeps you enslaved in your addiction. This is what interferes with your ability to attach and bond to your wife. If you don't understand this process and God's design for healthy intimacy in the marriage, you will remain imprisoned by your addiction.

Christ came to give you life and to set you free with the truth. There is hope. Science has finally caught up with what Paul wrote about in Romans 12:2—our brain can be transformed; our mind can be renewed! This week, we will continue to explore the battlefield of the brain and the practical application steps for renewing your mind.

Prayer for Change

Heavenly Father, thank You for creating in me such a wonderful and complex mind. Although I have not always used it to serve Your purpose in my life, I pray that You will perform a miracle in me and renew my mind. Thank You for giving me the patience I will need during this process. Help me to honor You in my mind. In Jesus' name, amen.

EPISODE 4 – Lesson Overview

Synthetic Attraction: Some years ago, male and female Gypsy Moths were brought into the United States with the intent of developing an amazing silk industry. However, instead of mating and creating a silk industry, they busied themselves by eating all the trees, which was disastrous. The scientists worked very hard to get rid of the Gypsy Moths. They developed various pesticides, but nothing worked. Then one scientist suggested creating a synthetic, but intense, form of the female scent. The male Gypsy Moth would then seek after the smell of the female Gypsy Moth. During mating season, with plenty of females to choose from, the male searched for his perfect female, but could never find her. Eventually, they couldn't mate and all the Gypsy Moths died. The male Gypsy Moth was looking for the synthetic smell—not the real smell of the one right in front of him. In essence, this is exactly what has happened with pornography.

The way God designed you is: whatever you're beholding at the point of sexual release, you literally glue to, attach to, hunger for, and will crave again. — **Dr. Doug Weiss**

Oxytocin and Vasopressin are "bonding" hormones that promote monogamy in sexual relationships. Women mainly produce oxytocin, while men produce vasopressin with small amounts of oxytocin. Oxytocin teaches us to forget, by separating the pain from the pleasure. Outside of God's will, these hormones will impair our judgment. In a marriage relationship, these hormones bond you to your partner during sexual release. These same chemicals are released while watching porn or during fantasy and bond you with the images. These images become your sexual triggers.

NOTES:

_____

_____

_____

_____

_____

Pornography damages the brain: Brain scans reveal clear similarities between a cocaine addict's brain and a porn addict's brain. Repeated viewing of pornography damages the pleasure centers, sears the conscience, and makes a person attracted to what is synthetic rather than what is real. It physically alters the structure of the brain. The only way to reverse the damage is by going through the process of renewing the mind.

A brain problem: When we examine the science behind sexual bondage, it is evident that we are dealing mainly with a brain issue, not a moral issue. Sexual bondage starts out as a moral problem (the baited hook analogy) and ends up becoming a brain problem. However, this doesn't take responsibility away from the sex addict. He is still responsible and held accountable for his decisions and actions.

That's the power of sexual bondage: it promises you everything, but gives you absolutely nothing. — **Dr. Ted Roberts**

Hope for healing: In Romans 12:2, the Apostle Paul wrote, "...be transformed by the renewing of your mind." Science is now confirming what the Bible already recorded over 2000 years ago. Now that we have discovered neuroplasticity, the brain's ability to change throughout life, we know that it is possible to physically restructure our brain by renewing it spiritually through the ministry of the Holy Spirit and by taking conscious steps to change our thinking. When our minds are renewed, our actions will naturally be consistent with our thought life.

Tools to Conquer: Group Confidentiality.

There are two options in this battle: we can either restrain or retrain. Now, restrain is the old approach—try harder! Restraining won't work. The only answer that works is that you have to retrain your brain - try smarter! And you can't do that alone. You're going to need a trainer; someone to help you.

NOTES:

_____

_____

_____

_____

The importance of a mentor: It's important to grasp that we cannot win this battle alone. We need our brothers-in-arms to keep us accountable and to strengthen us on our journey, but we also need godly mentors who will disciple us. It's important to find a mentor who understands the process of overcoming sexual bondage.

Evaluate yourself: Make sure that you have taken the SAST, either online (ConquerSeries. com/sast) or in the appendix of this study guide. Note the four indicators of sexual bondage:

1. Are you involved in a binge-purge cycle?

_____

2. Have you tried to stop but cannot?

_____

3. Do you lie to cover up your behavior?

_____

4. Do you have a sense of guilt about your behavior or are you living in contradiction to what you believe?

_____

_____

Tools to Conquer: Group Confidentiality.

Some of you may be saying right now, "I'm not going to share all my deepest, darkest secrets to my small group." In your group, you will make a commitment to confidentiality and a commitment to not share anything outside of the group that was shared inside the group. Once you take the step of opening-up, you'll discover you're not the only one struggling. Through growth and confidentiality, you'll learn to trust the guys in your group.

NOTES:

_____

_____

_____

_____

_____

Handling disclosure: Do not disclose your problem to your wife until after you've had at least six months of sobriety, or you will risk re-traumatizing her. Based on the experience of group leaders and members who have successfully gone through the Conquer Series, we recommend that you go through the Series once more after you have completed the entire course. This Series is packed with so much information that it usually takes a second round to digest it. Once you "graduate" from the Conquer Series, remain in an accountability group such as a Warpath group. The Warpath Series will take you much further in-depth on the topics discussed in the Conquer Series and help you on this new path to living a life of sexual integrity. The men in your group will be able to help you when the time comes for disclosure. But at some point, no matter the cost, your wife needs to know everything. This is integral to your healing and freedom.

Note: For those of you who have already disclosed your behaviors to your wife, we recommend that you continue to be open and honest with her. From our experience, many wives become frustrated when their husbands stop sharing once they enter a Conquer Group. Although you want to avoid any form of staggered disclosure—retraumatizing her with sporadic new information—continue to share what you are learning about your behavior to reinforce and build trust in the marriage.

Discussion

Watch Episode 4 of the Conquer Series before answering the following questions:

1. When we say that sexual bondage is mainly a brain problem, does it mean that a man in sexual bondage shouldn't be held responsible for his actions? Why or why not?

_____

_____

2. Romans 12:2 says: "Do not conform to the pattern of this world, but be transformed by the renewing of your mind." Knowing now that your brain is pliable until death (neuroplasticity), name some spiritual and practical things you can do to renew your mind and begin creating new neural pathways.

_____

_____

3. What is the benefit and wisdom of waiting at least six months before fully disclosing your addiction to your wife? What is involved in properly disclosing your addiction to your wife, or your significant other if you are not married, but in a serious relationship?

_____

_____

Accountability

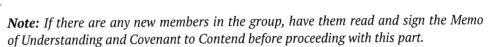

Note: If there are any new members in the group, have them read and sign the Memo of Understanding and Covenant to Contend before proceeding with this part.

Last week's 7-Day Mission

1. Last week we took an in-depth look at the FASTER Scale; identifying the various levels and behaviors that move us from restoration toward relapse. In light of this new information, were you better equipped to recognize your behaviors?

_____

_____

2. What was the lowest level you reached on the FASTER Scale last week? Did you call someone in your Conquer Group when you observed yourself sliding toward relapse? Share your experience with the group.

_____

_____

3. How did you do in journaling your battles during the week?

_____

_____

4. Were you able to call each member of your Conquer Group this past week?

_____

_____

5. How did you do preparing for battle each night? Did you face any specific challenges? Share your experience with the group.

_____

_____

Your 7-Day Mission – Week 4

1. FULL DISCLOSURE

Dr. Roberts asked each man to provide a full disclosure to his Conquer Group. Disclosure is a process that is explored in much greater depth in the Warpath Series, but this is a good start. Each person should fully disclose the general struggles of his addiction with his group members - not his wife.

Read this section out loud and fill out the Disclosure Table during your group meeting.

Please honor these guidelines in disclosing to your Conquer Group:
- Stick with information sharing; do not seek to justify or minimize any of your behaviors.
- Only disclose your facts and issues; do not share your wife's or significant other's information.
- Include the type of sexual acts that involve non-physical behaviors, such as fantasy, flirting, or plans to act out.
- Share the types of pornography you have looked at and the frequency of your pornography use.
- List the general type of sexual behavior that involved other people.
- Are there any other non-sexual addictive issues in your life? Unhealthy habits that include alcohol, drugs, food, finances, gambling, or others?
- Disclose to the best of your knowledge the financial cost of your addiction over the years (travel costs, purchases, missed work).
- Concerning felony sexual crimes: Know the laws in your state involving mandatory reporting before sharing with your group.

Remember that the group leaders and/or members may be mandatory state or federal reporters, and will not be able to maintain complete confidentiality if you disclose illegal activity.

Disclosure Table Example

BEHAVIORS	THE FACTS	FREQUENCY / COST
Fantasy, Flirting, or Plans to Act Out	• Sexually objectifying women at work and school • Fantasies of sexual encounters I would like to have, or from my past • Flirting with co-workers • Fantasies at night before going to sleep	Daily 3-5 times a week Daily Almost daily
Pornography	• Heterosexual intercourse and oral sex • Group sex: intercourse and oral sex • Lesbian	Once a week Once a month Occasionally
Physically Acting Out	• Three affairs: intercourse, oral sex, kissing • Masturbation	Over a 10 year period 4-5 times a week
Other Addictions	• Alcohol, smoking, food	Most of my life
Financial Costs of My Addictive Lifestyle	• Affairs (meals, presents, weekend away) • Alcohol and smoking • Porn (magazines, videos, clubs, gas) • Trip to Mexico with mistress	$55,000 $7,000 $2,500 $3,500

The process of creating a disclosure table will take time and intention. Most men in sexual bondage lie about their behavior. In order to lie to others, we must first lie to ourselves. This is why many addicts find that as they begin to work on the disclosure table, they will recall details that had been entirely blocked from their memory. As you gain sobriety, you will begin to remember more details about your behavior, details you may not be able to recall now. Eventually, you will need to fully disclose your behavior to the important people in your life. Completing this table, and being honest with yourself and your Conquer Group, is the first step in the disclosure process. As memories return, come back to this assignment and continue to add to the table.

During your group time, write down as many of the behaviors as you can and share with the group what you have identified. These boundaries will help you in this process:

1. *Use correct anatomical terminology when describing sexual behavior.*
2. *Avoid slang terms to describe sexual acts—refrain from using euphemisms.*
3. *Do not go into details about specific acts; simply describe the behavior. If you are concerned that something you are going to share could be triggering for other men in the group, talk about this with your group leader before the group meets.*

My Disclosure Table

BEHAVIORS	THE FACTS	FREQUENCY / COST
Fantasy, Flirting, or Plans to Act Out		
Pornography		
Physically Acting Out		
Other Addictions		
Financial Costs of My Addictive Lifestyle		

2. CALL EACH MEMBER IN YOUR CONQUER GROUP

Use the Call Schedule in your Conquer Series Journal to maintain connection with the other men in your Conquer Group. This is an essential step in breaking isolation, bringing you back into community with others.

3. JOURNAL YOUR BATTLES

Setting aside time each day to journal what you're going through—your struggles and your victories—can bring to light new perspectives and insights regarding your addictive behaviors. Remember, the more you understand where the behavior comes from, the better equipped you are to fight and win this battle. Be prepared to share what you're learning about yourself with the other members of your Conquer Group.

4. PREPARE FOR BATTLE EACH NIGHT

Every night, practice the following disciplines:

- Turn off all electronic devices 30 minutes before you go to sleep.
- Spend 10 minutes practicing deep diaphragmic breathing. This calms your limbic system, or what Scripture refers to as your heart.
- Spend 20 minutes doing something edifying in the Holy Spirit—meditating on Scripture and allowing the Holy Spirit into your heart each night.

5. USE THE FASTER SCALE IN YOUR CONQUER SERIES JOURNAL

The FASTER Scale in your Conquer Series Journal will help you identify where you are at on a daily basis. It is imperative that you make an honest and accurate self-assessment of your behaviors. The goal is to recognize where you are at and the direction you are headed, so you can change direction before relapse occurs. Connect with the members of your Conquer Group when you need support.

7-Day Mission Checklist – Week 4

Note: *The 7-Day Mission provides a concise weekly battle plan built on the key concepts in the episode for you to work out in your Conquer Series Study Guide and Journal. Additional exercises mentioned in the Conquer Series are suggestions for you to add on your own.*

☐ Filled out the Disclosure Table throughout the week; I am prepared to share my answers with my group next week

☐ Called each member in my Conquer Group

☐ Journaled my battles daily

☐ Prepared for battle each night

☐ Used the FASTER Scale daily in my Conquer Series Journal

Strongholds of the Enemy – Part 1

Strongholds of the Enemy – Part 1

Week 5, Episode 5

This lesson is based on Episode 5 of the Conquer Series. Read this introduction before watching Episode 5 and attending your Conquer Group.

For though we live in the world, we do not wage war as the world does. The weapons we fight with are not the weapons of the world. On the contrary, they have divine power to demolish strongholds. We demolish arguments and every pretension that sets itself up against the knowledge of God, and we take captive every thought to make it obedient to Christ. - 2 Corinthians 10:3-5

It is a serious thing when one's eyes have been opened to the truth, because with truth comes freedom. If Satan can keep a toehold of deception in your life to stop you from breaking completely free, he will do it; bound Christians cannot fight. This is what sexual bondage is all about: keeping a man in chains through deception, through the lies that have been mixed with the truth.

Many Christians never reach their full spiritual potential. They never reach the point of becoming weapons of war in God's hand because they have never conquered the strongholds in their lives: They remain spiritual pygmies. Because sexual bondage is mainly a battle of the mind, it is important that we learn to use God's weapons and take every thought captive, making it obedient to Christ. This allows us to prevail against the sin that so easily entangles. One of the greatest weapons we have is God's truth. Knowing the truth and getting that truth down into your soul is what brings change and freedom. To know the truth isn't just a point of head knowledge; it's relational, it's intimate, and it's a condition of the heart that is expressed in action.

In this lesson you will learn how you developed your arousal template—from both biological and environmental influences—and how the enemy can use it against you. Most sex addicts have a deep wound in their soul; you will learn how to access and understand your woundedness, so true healing can take place. You will also learn more about reprogramming the limbic system and the practical application steps needed to move toward health and freedom.

Prayer for Change

Father in Heaven, I pray that the Holy Spirit will reveal any deception in my life that has caused me to remain in bondage. Shed light on the dark places in my life, areas that no one can seem to reach, not even those who love me the most. Cleanse and soften my heart and help me to renew my mind so that You can use me. Regardless of how difficult this process may be or how long it takes, I commit myself into Your loving hands. Thank You that I have a Father in You. I pray this in Jesus' name, amen.

EPISODE 5 – Lesson Overview

Two strongholds the enemy can use:

1. First is the arousal template. Your arousal template is what turns you on sexually. It is uniquely individual. It's a mixture of your genetic background, your family of origin, and your sexual experiences. It's what you have learned to glue yourself to sexually.

2. Second, the enemy uses your wounds. Most people in sexual bondage have wounds that were typically caused during childhood or adolescence. However, not everyone in sexual bondage has major wounds; they can just feel under stress and find themselves acting out to medicate the pain. In other words, they have developed destructive coping mechanisms.

Anger is a secondary emotion. What you're primarily dealing with is fear. Men would really get healed if they faced their fears because the sense of worthlessness is chewing away at the individual's soul. — **Dr. Ted Roberts**

Tools to Conquer: The Arousal Template.

You may be asking, "Why is my arousal template important?" Without a correct understanding of the arousal template you personally have in your head, you will never have an effective relapse prevention plan. It's a tool that will help you conquer and prevent relapse from occurring in your life. Secondly, it will keep you from being blindsided by the enemy. Thirdly, it will keep you from crashing and not knowing why.

NOTES:

_____

_____

_____

_____

_____

_____

SUMMARY POINTS
- An arousal template is a form of sexual imprinting that you automatically return to.
- Your arousal template is uniquely individual.
- The more the sexual stimulus is repeated, the stronger the template will become.
- You must know your arousal template and trauma profile in order to create an effective relapse prevention plan.

The heart of bondage: When we refer to our "heart," we're actually referring to our limbic system. Most of the decisions we make are done on an unconscious level. When we are under a lot of pressure, the limbic system fires off, overpowering the prefrontal cortex. People in sexual bondage medicate their pain without their awareness.

Family of origin: We carry our family of origin with us in our brain. Often, you'll find father or mother wounds in people who struggle with sexual bondage. Sexual bondage is the result of panicking limbically. In other words, you act out because you're fearful about your worthlessness, which was imprinted during your formative years.

Fear—the root of selfishness: Selfishness is fear-driven. We are born wired with a need to survive that drives us into selfish behavior and the exploitation of others. Fear impairs our sense of unity and closeness with others. We have more apprehension and become more self-oriented.

NOTES:

_____

_____

_____

_____

_____

_____

_____

SUMMARY POINTS
- Most of our decisions are made on a subconscious level, in the limbic system.
- The limbic system is what the Bible refers to as our heart and our flesh.
- Fear hinders the prefrontal cortex from making rational decisions.
- Bondage takes place in the limbic system—our subconscious mind.

Tools to Conquer: Reprogram your limbic system.

Why is the limbic system the core of our addictive behavior? For two reasons: Firstly, it's programmed by the time you're six years old. Your prefrontal cortex (your braking or impulse-control system) isn't developed until you're twenty-five years old. Ninety-eight to ninety-nine percent of the decisions you make in life are done subconsciously; you're being directed by patterns of the past. Secondly, the limbic system is programmed to help you cope and survive, and coping behavior is at the core of addictive behavior. Sexual bondage is taking defective coping mechanisms and making them a lifestyle. In-depth healing comes from reprogramming your limbic system through the power of the Holy Spirit by God's Word; penetrating down into your soul, transforming you from the inside out.

Destructive vows: Vows result when the enemy takes our imagination captive. We only see the worst and live our life in light of what was done to us. That begins to affect our ability to dream and see what God wants to do in the future. Destructive vows have to be renounced so that we can start dreaming the dreams of God, instead of living in the past. Not all vows are destructive. We can make positive vows, but it's the destructive vows that can keep us in bondage.

Accessing the wound: Wounds create an intimacy disorder. Overreacting is one clear sign of a wound. Another indicator is if you can't tell your story. Once you discover the wounds in your soul, you'll discover the limbic lie that's been inserted into the place where you've been wounded.

Emotional wounds typically come from three sources. 1) Things people do to us. 2) Things people take from us. 3) Our own sins. We've been wounded by The Fall. We've been wounded by our own sin and by the sin of others. Here are my choices: I can either get into a process and experience healing of those wounds and receive the fullness and an abundance of intimate relationships with people, or I can refuse to experience healing, keep people at a distance, and try to medicate the pain. — **James Reeves**

NOTES:

_____

_____

_____

SUMMARY POINTS

- Sexual bondage is a coping mechanism to medicate wounds and to deal with the stress of life.
- Sexual bondage is panicking limbically.
- Typically, men in bondage have been deeply wounded by their earthly fathers.

Discussion

Watch Episode 5 of the Conquer Series before answering the following questions:

1. Dr. Ted Roberts says, "We carry our family of origin with us in our brain." What do you think about that statement? Is this evident in your life?

_____

_____

2. What destructive vows have you made at a time when you were wounded? First, identify a time when you were wounded, maybe something that happened when you were a child. Then, think about how you dealt with the wound. Did you make a statement (vow) such as, "I will never..."?

   Examples: I will never allow myself to be in an intimate relationship again. I'm never going to let anyone hurt me again (physically or sexually).

_____

_____

3. Dr. James Reeves says that emotional wounds come from three sources:
   1) things people do to us;
   2) things people take from us; and
   3) our own sins. Does this definition help you identify emotional wounds from your past in a new light?
   Does it offer you a new perspective regarding emotional wounds?

_____

_____

Accountability

Note: *If there are any new members in the group, have them read and sign the Memo of Understanding and Covenant to Contend before proceeding with this part.*

Last week's 7-Day Mission

1. Last week you were asked to provide a full disclosure to your Conquer Group. How did it go? Were you able to give a thorough account of your sexual history? Were there more details or events that came to mind during the week?

_____

_____

2. Did you call each member of your Conquer Group this week?

_____

_____

3. Did you make time to journal your battles on a daily basis? What were the struggles you encountered? What victories can we celebrate with you? Were you able to recognize anything new about your behaviors?

_____

_____

4. How successful were you in preparing for battle each night? What was most challenging? What is getting easier about preparing for battle each night?

_____

_____

5. What was the lowest level you reached on the FASTER Scale this week? Did you call someone in your Conquer Group to help you avoid relapse?

_____

_____

Your 7-Day Mission – Week 5

1. DISCOVER YOUR AROUSAL—RELAPSE CONNECTION

It is important that you understand how arousal contributes to relapse. This week, in your Conquer Series Journal, fill in the table provided—My Last Relapse Table—to gain new insights into your acting out behaviors.

2. MY 10 WORST MOMENTS

In the following table, list the 10 worst moments of your life. Then, identify any vows you made as a result of those moments. All of us have experienced painful events. Recognizing the impact that those events had in our lives and their contribution to our addictive behaviors can help us begin to break the chains of bondage.

My 10 Worst Moments

IN THE BOXES BELOW, LIST THE 10 WORST MOMENTS OF YOUR LIFE.	IDENTIFY ANY VOWS YOU MADE AS A RESULT OF YOUR WORST MOMENTS.
Example: When I was in high school, I embarrassed myself with my girlfriend.	1. I will never again be vulnerable with women.
Example: My parents' divorce.	1. I will never trust the important people in my life. 2. I will never get married.
1.	
2.	
3.	
4.	
5.	
6.	
7.	
8.	
9.	
10.	

Analysis:
Looking at the vows you made as a result of your worst moments, is there a commonality or theme you can identify?

Now, look at the answers you provided on the Last Relapse Table in your *Conquer Series Journal*. Are any of the actions or steps that contributed to your relapse as the result of a vow you made when experiencing one of the worst moments in your life? Do you recognize any connection between vows you have made and your relapse?

3. THE DOUBLE BIND EXERCISE

Many people who struggle with addictive behaviors are continually faced with difficult choices to make. Throughout the day, perhaps several times a day, they find themselves at a crossroad; they have a decision to make and all their options lead to a negative consequence. They are faced with a double bind.[1]

A double bind is a lose/lose situation that often involves risk and fear. We've all heard the saying, "Stuck between a rock and a hard place." This saying sums-up a double bind. The challenge we face is choosing the lesser of two evils; making a choice that may result in immediate consequences, but will inevitably benefit us. For example, if I tell my wife about my pornography use and masturbation, she will feel angry, hurt, and betrayed. But, I also can't continue living a lie; the guilt and shame I feel on a daily basis is eating me up inside. This is a lose/lose situation. I have a difficult choice to make. I can risk telling my wife the truth and suffer the consequences of hurting her OR I can keep quiet and continue to carry the weight of my sin, trapped by my own fear. If I tell my wife about my behavior, although it will hurt her, I will be free from this secret and have the opportunity to restore my marriage OR I can continue to lie to her and try to stop my behaviors on my own. This is a double bind.

When faced with a double bind, the struggle is not with identifying the right thing to do. We know what the right choice is; we know what we should do. However, that doesn't make the choice any easier because of the risk and fear involved. If we choose to do the right thing, we give up something; we have to make a change. If we don't change, or choose to ignore the problem, then we are choosing to stay a prisoner to our addiction. As Michael Dye has said, "The right thing to do is usually the hard thing to do."[2]

This week, your 7-Day Mission includes the following double bind exercise.[3] In the space below, work through a few recent situations where you experienced a double bind as a result of your addictive behaviors. Answer the corresponding questions pertaining to the specific situation and the choices you made. Follow up by determining the "right thing to do" and the strategies to help you succeed.

Example:

Situation/Issue: *I was recently "friended" by an old high school girlfriend on Facebook. We have been chatting on Facebook and texting for the past month. It started off casually, but has escalated to sexual conversations. She wants to have an affair. Initially I felt excitement, but now I struggle with feelings of guilt and shame.*

Choice #1—*Necessary change: I love my wife and know this relationship would hurt her. I really should tell her about it and break it off with my old girlfriend. If I tell my wife, it will damage our relationship, possibly beyond repair. I know she will feel betrayed and not trust me.*

Choice #2—*No change: I can maintain a friendship with my old girlfriend. It won't go any further than that. If I keep my interactions with her to a minimum, my wife will never know. I can manage the guilt and shame I feel. This is not really a betrayal.*

The right thing to do: *I need to tell my wife and discontinue my relationship with my old girlfriend. I know there will be consequences, but I can't continue to live a lie.*

Strategies for success: *I will meet with my pastor for advice before telling my wife. I will limit my Facebook friends to male friends only. I will do whatever my wife needs me to do, so that she can feel safe and so that we can begin to build trust in our marriage.*

Your Turn

Situation/Issue:

_____

_____

Choice #1—necessary change:

_____

_____

Choice #2—no change:

_____

_____

The right thing to do:

_____

_____

Strategies for success:

_____

_____

Situation/Issue:

_____

_____

Choice #1 — necessary change:

_____

_____

Choice #2 — no change:

_____

_____

The right thing to do:

_____

_____

Strategies for success:

_____

_____

Situation/Issue:

_____

_____

Choice #1 — necessary change:

_____

_____

Choice #2—no change:

_____

_____

The right thing to do:

_____

_____

Strategies for success:

_____

_____

Processing a double bind can be challenging. It can feel emotionally exhausting and can bring up feelings that you have kept hidden for many years. However, it is a tool that you must master; it will help you identify the behaviors that lead to relapse. As you work through this week's double bind exercise, pay close attention to where you're at on the FASTER Scale. If you find yourself sliding down the FASTER Scale, identify the double bind you're facing and work through it. Practicing this double bind exercise on a regular basis will help you to be more aware of what drives your addiction and how to avoid relapse.

One final note: As you use the tools you've been given to process your addictive behaviors and move toward healing, watch out for HALT. When you're feeling Hungry, Angry, Lonely or Tired, the enemy will use this to set you up; pulling you away from health and driving you deeper into your addiction. This is the danger zone. If you feel this happening, call one of the men in your Conquer Group for support.

4. USE THE FASTER SCALE IN YOUR CONQUER SERIES JOURNAL

The FASTER Scale in your Conquer Series Journal will help you identify where you are at on a daily basis. It is imperative that you make an honest and accurate self-assessment of your behaviors. The goal is to recognize where you are at and the direction you are headed, so you can change direction before relapse occurs. Connect with the members of your Conquer Group when you need support.

[1] Dye, M. (2012). The Genesis Process: For Change Groups, Book 1 and 2, Individual Workbook. Auburn, CA: Michael Dye. 57.
[2] Ibid. 270.
[3] Dye, M. (2012). The Genesis Process: For Change Groups, Book 1 and 2, Individual Workbook. Auburn, CA: Michael Dye. Adapted and used with permission.

7-Day Mission Checklist – Week 5

Note: *The 7-Day Mission provides a concise weekly battle plan built on the key concepts in the episode for you to work out in your Conquer Series Study Guide and Journal. Additional exercises mentioned in the Conquer Series are suggestions for you to add on your own.*

☐ Reviewed my arousal template looking for specific patterns that lead to relapse

☐ Completed my 10 Worst Moments Table; I am prepared to share with my Conquer Group

☐ Completed the Double Bind Exercise in my Conquer Series Journal

☐ Used the FASTER Scale daily in my Conquer Series Journal

We have reached the end of Volume 1. I hope that you will continue this journey by moving on to Volume 2; you and the other men in your Conquer Group. The next five episodes focus on the weapons and strategies that God has given you in preparation for this battle. I've used these same strategies to help thousands of men break free from sexual addiction. It's packed with new information and practical application steps intended to move you closer to becoming who God called you to be. Join me in the next level of your journey toward freedom. Let's finish what we started together, finding strength and honor in Christ.

God bless you,

Dr. Ted Roberts

Appendix

Sexual Addiction Screening Test (SAST)

The Sexual Addiction Screening Test (SAST) is designed to assist in the assessment of sexually compulsive or "addictive" behavior. Developed in cooperation with hospitals, treatment programs, private therapists, and community groups, the SAST provides a profile of responses that help to discriminate between addictive and non-addictive behavior. To complete the test, answer each question by circling the appropriate yes/no response.

Yes No 1. Were you sexually abused as a child or adolescent?

Yes No 2. Did your parents have trouble with sexual behavior?

Yes No 3. Do you often find yourself preoccupied with sexual thoughts?

Yes No 4. Do you feel that your sexual behavior is not normal?

Yes   No 5. Do you ever feel bad about your sexual behavior?

Yes No 6. Has your sexual behavior ever created problems for you and your family?

Yes No 7. Have you ever sought help for sexual behavior you did not like?

Yes No 8. Has anyone been hurt emotionally because of your sexual behavior?

Yes No 9. Are any of your sexual activities against the law?

Yes No 10. Have you made efforts to quit a type of sexual activity and failed?

Yes No 11. Do you hide some of your sexual behaviors from others?

Yes No 12. Have you attempted to stop some parts of your sexual activity?

Yes No 13. Have you felt degraded by your sexual behaviors?

Yes No 14. When you have sex, do you feel depressed afterwards?

Yes No 15. Do you feel controlled by your sexual desire?

Yes No 16. Have important parts of your life (such as job, family, friends, leisure activities) been neglected because you were spending too much time on sex?

Yes No 17. Do you ever think your sexual desire is stronger than you are?

Yes No 18. Is sex almost all you think about?

Yes No 19. Has sex (or romantic fantasies) been a way for you to escape your problems?

Yes No 20. Has sex become the most important thing in your life?

Yes No 21. Are you in crisis over sexual matters?

Yes No 22. The Internet has created sexual problems for me.

Yes No 23. I spend too much time online for sexual purposes.

Yes No 24. I have purchased services online for erotic purposes (sites for dating, pornography, fantasy and friend finder).

Yes No 25. I have used the Internet to make romantic or erotic connections with people online.

Yes No 26. People in my life have been upset about my sexual activities online.

Yes No 27. I have attempted to stop my online sexual behaviors.

Yes No 28. I have subscribed to or regularly purchased or rented sexually explicit materials (magazines, videos, books or online pornography).

Yes No 29. I have been sexual with minors.

Yes No 30. I have spent considerable time and money on strip clubs, adult bookstores and movie houses.

Yes No 31. I have engaged prostitutes and escorts to satisfy my sexual needs.

Yes   No   32. I have spent considerable time surfing pornography online.

Yes   No   33. I have used magazines, videos or online pornography even when there was considerable risk of being caught by family members who would be upset by my behavior.

Yes   No   34. I have regularly purchased romantic novels or sexually explicit magazines.

Yes   No   35. I have stayed in romantic relationships after they became emotionally abusive.

Yes   No   36. I have traded sex for money or gifts.

Yes   No   37. I have maintained multiple romantic or sexual relationships at the same time.

Yes   No   38. After sexually acting out, I sometimes refrain from all sex for a significant period.

Yes   No   39. I have regularly engaged in sadomasochistic behavior.

Yes   No   40. I visit sexual bath-houses, sex clubs or video/bookstores as part of my regular sexual activity.

Yes   No   41. I have engaged in unsafe or "risky" sex even though I knew it could cause me harm.

Yes   No   42. I have cruised public restrooms, rest areas, or parks looking for sex with strangers.

Yes   No   43. I believe casual or anonymous sex has kept me from having more long-term intimate relationships.

Yes   No   44. My sexual behavior has put me at risk for arrest for lewd conduct or public indecency.

Yes   No   45. I have been paid for sex.

SAST – R v2.0
© 2008, P. J. Carnes, Sexual Addiction Screening Test – Revised

SAST (Sexual Addiction Screening Test) Scoring

SCALES	ITEM #	CUT-OFF (NUMBER OF "YES" RESPONSES). MORE THAN THE CUT-OFF NUMBER INDICATES A CONCERN IN THIS AREA	HOW MANY "YES" RESPONSES DID I HAVE?
Core item scale	1-20	6 or more	
Subscales			
Internet Items	22-27	3 or more	
Men's Items	28-33	2 or more	
Women's Items	34-39	2 or more	
Homosexual Men	40-45	3 or more	
Addictive Dimensions			
Preoccupation	3, 18, 19, 20	2 or more	
Loss of Control	10, 12, 15, 17	2 or more	
Relationship Disturbance	6, 8, 16, 26	2 or more	
Affect Disturbance	4, 5, 11, 13, 14	2 or more	

Relative Distributions of Addict & Non-Addict SAST Scores. This instrument has been based on screenings of tens of thousands of people. This particular version is a developmental stage revision of the instrument, so scoring may be adjusted with more research. Please be aware that clinical decisions must be made conditionally since final scoring protocols may vary.

The Bible And Sexual Sin

Among Christians, there is much confusion regarding sexual sin. The explanations below lists those "grey areas" that we hope will bring clarity to what is and is not biblically permissible.

MASTURBATION (SELF-SEX)

If you are masturbating in secret or substituting it for sex with your wife, then it is a sin and goes against biblical principles because:

- You become carnally minded. Masturbation is about self-gratification—it gratifies the flesh (Romans 8:5 and 2 Corinthians 3:1–5).
- It creates shame in your life, which leads to intimacy problems in your relationship with God and others.
- You become enslaved: The neurochemicals released during masturbation have the same addictive effect as drugs. Single men, who think that masturbation will help relieve their sexual desire before marriage, set themselves up for addiction that will continue in their marriage. Don't be deceived. If God is not enough for you when you're single, your wife will not be enough for you when you're married.
- You fantasize; it's almost impossible to masturbate without fantasizing, which creates strongholds in the mind.
- You violate God's purpose for sex, which is for procreation and pleasure by putting the other person's sexual needs and desires above your own. Masturbation eliminates both.
- You open the door to other sexual sins, such as pornography, premarital sex, adultery, and more.

ORAL SEX

Permissible within the covenant of marriage, but is considered fornication outside of marriage because it is a sexual act. Oral sex should only be with mutual consent and enjoyment—never a demand. In the Song of Solomon, God encourages married people to enjoy His gift of sex to the full. Some who have studied the Bible, such as Joseph Dillow (Solomon on Sex), think that "fruit" and "garden" references may be meant as metaphors for oral sex.

ANAL SEX

No scriptures specifically mention anal sex, but this doesn't mean that it is not a sin. Scripture is clear that your body belongs to God and is the temple of the Holy Spirit; as an act of worship, your body is to be presented to God as holy and acceptable.

1 Corinthians 6:16: Do you not know that your body is the temple of the Holy Spirit who is in you, whom you have received from God? You are not your own; you were bought with a price. Therefore honor God with your body.

Romans 12:1: Therefore, I urge you, brothers, in view of God's mercy to offer your bodies as living sacrifices, holy and pleasing to God—this is your spiritual act of worship.

The act of anal sex is referred to as sodomy, which the Bible condemns as an unnatural way to have intercourse. Hence, anal sex is defiling the marriage bed. Whenever you intentionally put your body at risk for harm and disease, you are dishonoring God's "temple."

Here are a few health reasons explaining the harmful effects of anal sex:
- The anus is full of bacteria. Penetration can tear the tissue inside the anus, allowing bacteria and viruses to enter the bloodstream. Having vaginal sex after anal sex can also lead to vaginal, bladder, and kidney infections.
- The anus was designed to hold in feces. Because the sphincter muscle was not designed to dilate continuously like the vagina, forced dilation can lead to future incontinence, which means repetitive anal sex can lead to a weakening of the anal sphincter, making it difficult to hold your bowels.
- Studies show that the person receiving anal sex often experiences shame and embarrassment which can lead to depression.

FANTASY
Whether you are married or single, sexual fantasy is sin. Jesus said, "But I say to you that whoever looks at a woman to lust for her has already committed adultery with her in his heart" (Matthew 5:28). When you fantasize sexually you "look" at a woman through the eye-gate of your mind and lust for her within your heart.

The Apostle Paul writes, "Finally, brothers and sisters, whatever is true, whatever is noble, whatever is right, whatever is pure, whatever is lovely, whatever is admirable—if anything is excellent or praiseworthy—think about such things" (Philippians 4:8). Fantasies are what Satan often uses to highjack and defile our minds. Furthermore, sexual fantasy often leads to masturbation and opens the door to premarital sex and adultery.

PETTING (TOUCHING YOUR PARTNER'S PRIVATE PARTS)
Permitted within marriage by mutual consent, but is a sin outside of marriage. In 1 Corinthians 7:1 (KJV), Scripture says, "It is good for a man not to touch a woman." One of the meanings for the Greek word for "touch" means "to press against in such a way as to kindle or catch on fire." So another way to translate this verse would be, "It is good for a man not to touch a woman so that they become sexually aroused."

Note: Some of the above information is adapted and/or summarized from the Marriage, Sexuality and Personal Development section from Probe Ministries: probe.org

Group Leader's Checklist

Before every meeting:

☐ Is your device hooked up and ready to play the episode?

☐ Is there good audio?

☐ Is the room arranged comfortably for conversation and discussion? Does everyone have a good view of the TV screen?

☐ Are there enough pens for everyone?

☐ Pray!

At the meeting:

☐ Ask any new group members to sign the Memo of Understanding and Covenant to Contend.

☐ As the leader, you set the tone for group interaction. If your responses to the Discussion and Accountability questions are truthful and honest, then others in your group will begin to trust and respond honestly.

☐ As the group facilitator, your role is to guide the group time and ask good questions that validate and encourage participation. You must balance the needs of the individual with the needs of the group as a whole.

☐ During the accountability session, allow time for a progress check on the previous week's 7-Day Mission.

☐ Close the meeting with prayer.

Discover More Online

ConquerSeries.com
facebook.com/conquerseries

VOLUNTEER
JOIN CONQUER 100

Dr. Ted Roberts Host of the Conquer Series

There are millions of men suffering in silence in their struggle with pornography, hoping to find a solution to break the bondage in their lives.

Help bring healing to churches in your area. Join Conquer 100 and pledge to introduce the Conquer Series to churches in your community. Register at ConquerSeries.com.

Dr. Ted Roberts is the host of the Conquer Series. This former marine fighter pilot and senior pastor is the founder and leader of Pure Desire Ministries Int'l, a ministry devoted to healing sexual addicts and their spouses, with a 90% success rate. A former sex addict himself, Dr. Roberts knows what it takes to conquer hell at close range. He has over 30 years of counseling experience helping men get free from sexual addiction and helping husbands and wives restore their marriages.

GET THE CONQUER SERIES
AND OTHER RESOURCES AT
CONQUERSERIES.COM

JOIN A CONQUER GROUP

The accountability group is your combat team where healing and freedom truly takes place. You cannot win this battle alone.

STEP 1: VISIT CONQUERSERIES.COM

STEP 2:
REGISTER FOR A
CONQUER GROUP

STEP 3:
MEET WITH YOUR
GROUP ONLINE
OR A LOCATION
NEAR YOU

"AS IRON SHARPENS IRON, ONE MAN SHARPENS ANOTHER."
PROVERBS 27:17

WATCH THE CONQUER SERIES
ONLINE!

The Conquer Series is now available digitally with instant viewing access on any of your internet-connected devices. Overcoming real struggles requires authentic and powerful teachings and NOW the Conquer Series is available on your TV, phone, iPad or computer to be viewed 24/7.

We've taken the entire Conquer Series along with a newly designed, Interactive Study Guide to bring you all the digital tools and resources necessary to live a life of sexual integrity.

Get Access Today
ConquerSeries.com
(561) 681-9990